AWESOME ATHLETES

GRANT HILL

Paul Joseph
ABDO & Daughters

visit us at
www.abdopub.com

Published by Abdo & Daughters, 4940 Viking Drive, Suite 622, Edina, Minnesota 55435. Copyright © 1998 by Abdo Consulting Group, Inc., Pentagon Tower, P.O. Box 36036, Minneapolis, Minnesota 55375 USA. International copyrights reserved in all countries. No part of this book may be reproduced in any form without written permission from the publisher.

Printed in the United States.

Cover and Interior Photo credits: Duomo
Allsports

Edited by Kal Gronvall

Library of Congress Cataloging-in-Publication Data

Joseph, Paul, 1970-
    Grant Hill / Paul Joseph.
    p. cm. -- (Awesome athletes)
    Includes index.
    Summary: A biography of the Duke University and Detroit Piston superstar whose many honors include an Olympic gold medal for playing on the 1996 United States Men's Basketball Team.
    ISBN 1-56239-843-1
    1. Hill, Grant--Juvenile literature. 2. Basketball players--United States--Biography--Juvenile literature. [1. Hill, Grant. 2. Basketball players. 3. Afro-Americans--Biography.] I. Title. II. Series.
    GV884.H55J67 1998   97-25809
    796.323'092--dc21   CIP
    [B]   AC

Contents

All-Around All-Star 4

Famous Parents 6

Growing Up 9

High School Star 11

The Blue Devil 13

Grant Wins A Championship 15

Off to the Motor City 20

The NBA Playoffs 22

A Gold Medal 24

Change The Game 26

King of the Hill 28

Glossary 30

Index 32

All-Around All-Star

Grant Hill is not only one of the greatest players in the **National Basketball Association (NBA)** and a two-time NBA **All-Star**, but he is an All-Star off the court as well. He is the dream of every mother, father, coach, teammate, fan, and friend.

Grant is an articulate, smart, overall nice guy. The Detroit Pistons' sensational six-foot, eight-inch forward easily leads the league in class and also plays the game with intensity and skill.

Grant believes in team over self, therefore, making him one of the best teammates a player could have. He believes in working hard, staying in school, respecting parents and coaches, and being a good friend.

In Grant's short pro career, the multi-talented player has already been named **Rookie of the Year**, started in three **All-Star Games**—getting the most votes twice, won a gold medal as part of the United States Dream Team, and led his team to the **playoffs**.

Grant is a true role model who doesn't shy away from responsibility. He has risen above the "trash talk" that takes place in sports and has proven that talent, teamwork, and practice are the ways to make it.

Young people can look up to Grant as one who stresses family values, integrity, and equality. He also helps young people through his countless **charities** and never refuses an **autograph** or talking with his fans.

Grant is truly in a league of his own, not only on the court but off the court as well. It took many years of hard work to get where he is today, and it started when he was a very young child.

Grant Hill of the Detroit Pistons.

Famous Parents

Grant Hill was born on October 5, 1972, in Dallas, Texas. He is the only child of Calvin and Janet Hill. His father Calvin was a star NFL running back. After becoming an All-American for Yale University, he was **drafted** by the Dallas Cowboys. Calvin won the **Rookie of the Year** Award and later captured a Super Bowl victory with the Cowboys.

His mother Janet **graduated** from Wellesley **College**, one of the top schools in the country. Janet's college roommate was First Lady Hillary Rodham Clinton. Janet pursued a career in politics. She worked in Washington, D.C., for the Pentagon and now is a partner in a consulting firm.

When Grant was born his parents couldn't come up with a name for him. For the first few days of his life they called him "Baby Boy Hill." His parents had a few names they liked but couldn't decide on one. Finally, the Hall of Fame quarterback of the Cowboys, Roger Staubach, who was a good friend of the family's said, "That's it. His name is Grant." And that is how Grant Hill got his name.

Grant's mom taught him to strive to be the best and always work hard in school. If he got a "B" in school and she knew he could get an "A," she would be very upset with him. "Never be satisfied with mediocrity," she would tell Grant.

Grant's father Calvin grew up in New York City. As a child he worked very hard in school and sports. After doing very well in high school, he received a **scholarship** to one of the best schools in the country, Yale University. There, again, he excelled in school and sports.

Calvin is the quiet one in the family. He made sure that his son worked hard but never pushed him. Calvin would show by action rather than words what hard work can accomplish. Calvin also had a very competitive nature that was passed on to Grant.

Grant's parents made sure that he had everything, but they also made sure that he worked for it. Grant's parents gave him all the love, patience, and understanding he needed to be a success in life.

Grant Hill's parents cheering him on at a game.

Growing Up

Grant loved many sports as a child. At the age of seven he dreamed of being a quarterback on the Dallas Cowboys like his idol Roger Staubach. He also played soccer, baseball, and of course basketball.

Grant and his parents moved to Virginia when he was a young child. They lived very close to Washington, D.C. As an only child, Grant received a lot of attention from both parents. They were very supportive of everything he did. But Grant also missed out on having brothers and sisters. Both of his parents were also only children, so Grant didn't have uncles, aunts, or cousins.

Grant, however, had a lot of friends, and the many sports that he played kept him very busy.

Grant was also taller than most of the kids his age, and the coach would always put him at **center**. Grant didn't like playing center because he didn't get to handle the ball very much. His dad finally told him to take charge. So Grant talked to the coach about changing positions. Soon Grant began bringing the ball up the court and shooting more as a guard and forward.

Grant had a childhood just like any American kid. He played with friends, played sports, went to the mall, went on vacations with his parents, and went to school. One thing set him apart, though. His father was a famous **athlete**.

Sometimes that was very hard for Grant to deal with. He didn't want people to think he was better just because his dad was famous. He wanted to be like every other kid. He was even embarrassed at times by his dad's success. In eighth grade his dad spoke at his school. Grant didn't want him to come, but when he did, Grant faked he was sick and went home.

Grant also asked his dad to drive his old beat-up VW Bug instead of one of his many nice cars when he would drop Grant off at school, practice, or the mall. Grant never wanted people to think he was showing off. His dad understood and always hopped into the Bug whenever Grant needed a ride.

High School Star

At the age of 14, Grant was six-feet, three-inches and the most talented basketball player in high school. He made the **varsity** basketball team as only a **freshman**.

Grant could play any position on the floor. He could shoot, pass, post-up, and usually guarded the best player on the other team. He also worked on his game more than most players. Grant would practice, work-out, and even study the game. For hours on end he would watch basketball videos just to learn how to play better ball.

In school, Grant was an honor student. His parents made sure that he studied and got good grades. Nothing was more important to his parents than a good education and Grant believed that too.

Grant never had to be told to study because he knew that at any moment an injury could end his career and he would need his education to fall back on. His dad told him many stories about great **athletes** who had nothing to fall back on because they either got hurt or didn't know how to manage their money. Grant even volunteered to tutor students who were struggling with school.

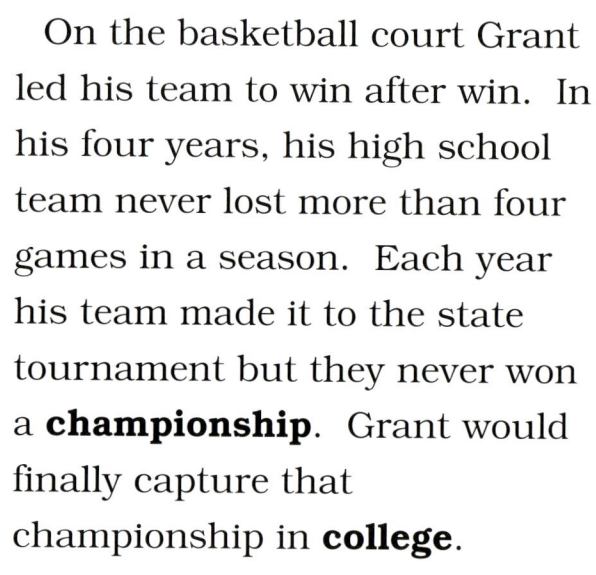

On the basketball court Grant led his team to win after win. In his four years, his high school team never lost more than four games in a season. Each year his team made it to the state tournament but they never won a **championship**. Grant would finally capture that championship in **college**.

Grant Hill playing college ball with the Duke Blue Devils.

The Blue Devil

In Grant's **senior** year in high school, he dominated. Grant averaged 30 points per game, 12 **rebounds**, and 8 assists. Every major **college** wanted this high school sensation to play on their team.

Georgetown, Louisville, North Carolina, UCLA, Duke, Michigan— they all wanted Grant, and they all offered him **scholarships**. Grant was sure he was going to Georgetown. The school was right in his back yard, he loved Coach John Thompson, and it was his favorite college team.

Then Grant thought about North Carolina. It had the great tradition of college basketball, led by Coach Dean Smith. It had also produced some of the greatest players in the game, including Michael Jordan.

Then there was Duke University. Grant hated Duke, he didn't even want to visit the school. But once he did, he knew that Duke was the place for him. The major reason was Coach Mike Krzyzewski, otherwise known as Coach K.

Every other coach told Grant that he would be a starter in his **freshman** year. Coach K told him that if he worked hard and deserved it he would play. But he wasn't going to guarantee anything to anyone. Coach K told Grant that he would have to earn his minutes and earn a starting spot.

Grant was hooked on Coach K's style of basketball and never looked at another school. Grant was a Duke Blue Devil.

Grant Hill (33) celebrating two championships in a row with his Duke teammates and Coach K.

Grant Wins A Championship

When Grant got to Duke he was no longer the star of the team. Duke already had a great team that was loaded with talent. They had Christian Laettner, Bobby Hurley, Thomas Hill, Brian Davis, and Cherokee Parks.

Grant, however, worked very hard and was a starter in his **freshman** year. He owed a lot of his success to Coach K. His coach taught him how to win. He said that in order to be a winner you must be focused, work hard, and prepare for each game. Grant listened to his coach and continued to watch videos to learn the game even better.

In Grant's freshman year in 1991, Duke had everything. They had great all-around players with size, quickness, great shooting ability, and played excellent team defense.

They ran through the **NCAA** tournament all the way to the Final Four. There, Grant finally got that

championship for which he was looking. The Duke Blue Devils were the best team in **college** basketball.

The following year Duke was even better. They had almost the entire team returning. And Grant was even better. They cruised through the regular season, dominating teams. The 1992 Duke team was one of the best teams in college history.

They always had the will to win and often times the magic. For example, in the **NCAA** tournament, with two seconds remaining, the Blue Devils were down by one point to Kentucky. From under the other basket, somehow Grant threw the ball right to Christian Laettner who was standing way at the other end of the floor near the free-throw line. He caught the perfect pass, turned, and put up a shot. His shot hit nothing but net for the game winner!

After that magical win no other team came close to beating Duke. Again, Duke was too much for the competition. The Blue Devils won back-to-back NCAA Championships.

The next season most of the team was gone. Grant Hill would have to do it on his own—and he did. Before the season started, Grant guaranteed another national **championship**. Some people didn't even think they could make it to the **NCAA** tournament. Grant, however, led his team all the way to the Final Four. It was quite an accomplishment for a team that had lost so many outstanding players.

The Blue Devils didn't win a third national championship but they came very close. In Grant's last year with the Blue Devils he again led them to the Final Four, but they lost the championship game.

In Grant's four years as a Blue Devil, the team went to the Final Four four times and won the national championship twice. In his last two seasons, Grant averaged nearly 20 points, 7 **rebounds**, and 8 assists. In his **senior** season he led the Blue Devils in scoring and assists and was a First Team All American. After a great four year **college** career every **NBA** team wanted Grant—but only one could have him.

THE MAKING OF AN AWESOME ATHLETE

Grant Hill stretching out before a game with the Pistons.

1972
Born October 5, in Dallas, TX. He is an only child.

1986
Plays for South Lakes High School as a freshman.

1989
Accepts scholarship to Duke University.

1992
Wins second straight title with Duke University.

How Awesome Is He?

Here is the list of his stats from the 1995-96 NBA season and how they compare to other players in the same season.

Player	Games	PPG	RPG
Clyde Drexler	52	19.3	7.2
Grant Hill	**80**	**20.2**	**9.8**
Jason Kidd	81	16.6	6.8
Larry Johnson	81	20.5	8.4
Michael Jordan	82	30.4	6.6
Scottie Pippen	77	19.4	6.4

GRANT HILL

TEAM: DETROIT PISTONS
NUMBER: 33
POSITION: FORWARD
HEIGHT: 6 FEET 8 INCHES
WEIGHT: 225 pounds

1994
Leads the Blue Devils in scoring and assists.

1994
Drafted third overall by the Detroit Pistons.

1995
Wins NBA Rookie of the Year scoring 1,394 points.

1995
Leading vote-getter in the NBA All-Star Game.

Highlights

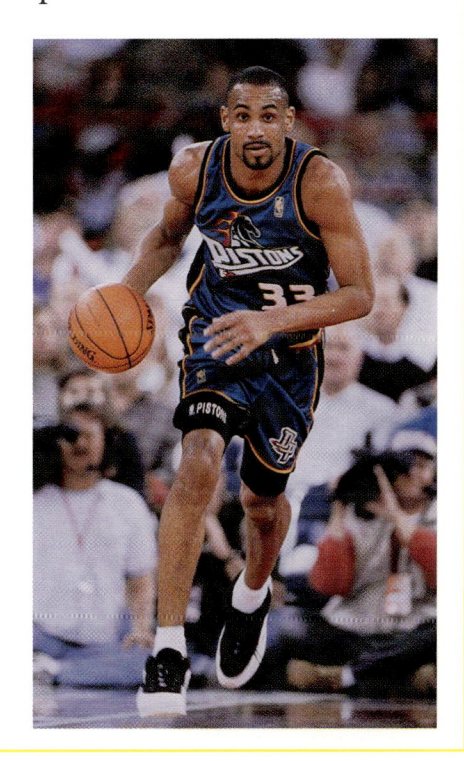

- Named College All-American three times.
- Led Duke University to two NCAA Championships.
- Named the 1995 NBA Rookie of the Year.
- Scored 1,394 points in his rookie year.
- Named to the NBA All-Star Team his first three years in the NBA.

Off to the Motor City

Grant could have left school early to join the **NBA**. He could have left after two years of **college**, made millions of dollars, and been an **All-Star**. Grant, however, knew that graduating from college was the most important thing in his life. He worked very hard to be the best basketball player and best student. As in high school, Grant tutored students in college who were struggling with their classes.

In 1994, the last place Detroit Pistons **drafted** Grant with the third overall pick in the NBA Draft. The six-foot, eight-inch forward signed a **contract** that paid him $45 million over 8 years!

The Detroit Pistons were making Grant Hill the franchise player—and Grant did not let them down. Grant was even better than everyone expected. He was the leading scorer with 20 points per game.

Grant was an immediate star and fan favorite. He was the first **rookie** ever to lead all players in fan voting for the **NBA All-Star Game**. At season's end he was named NBA co-**Rookie of the Year** along with Jason Kidd of the Dallas Mavericks.

Although the young, inexperienced team didn't win a lot of games, the fans were still excited about the future. The 1994-95 Pistons finished with a 28-54 record, but the following season would be a different story.

Grant Hill (L) and Clyde Drexler exchanging words on the court.

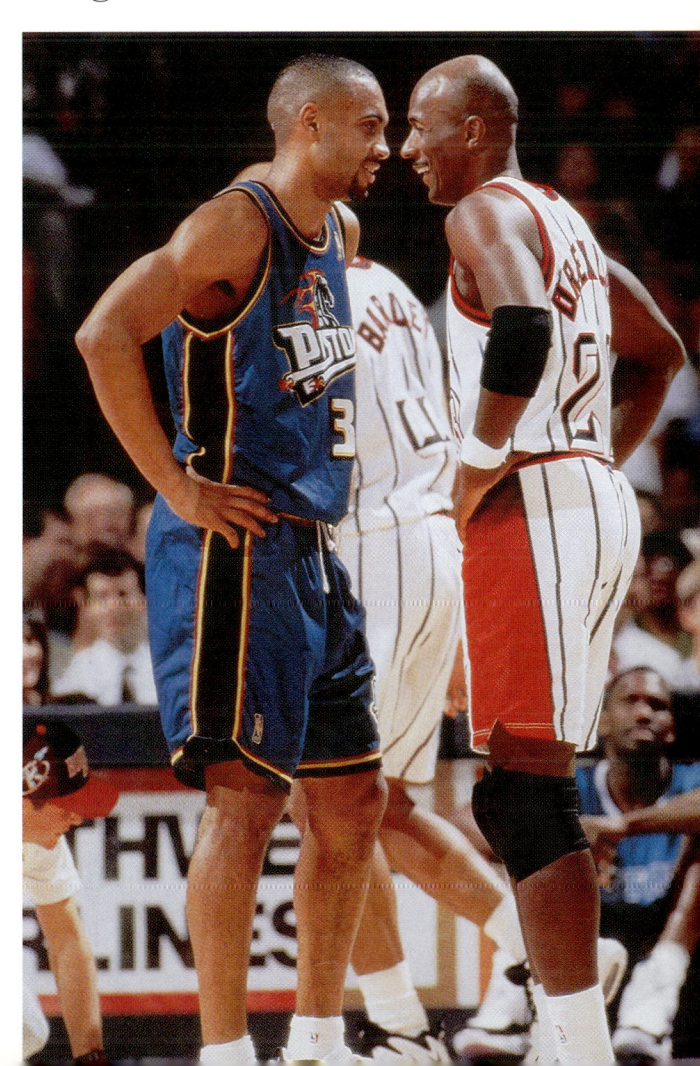

The NBA Playoffs

The Pistons came out in 1995-96 and nearly doubled their win total from the year before. Detroit finished with a 46-36 record and a spot in the **playoffs**.

The biggest reason for their success was Grant Hill. The second-year **All-Star** led his team in points, **rebounds**, and assists. Another reason for their success was new coach Doug Collins. Collins had known Grant very well because his son had played with Grant. He told Grant that he would have to be the team leader on offense, defense, and in the locker room.

Grant was under a lot of pressure, but he loved it. He made the Pistons a real force in the **NBA**. In the playoffs the Pistons were ousted by the Orlando Magic in the first round. Nevertheless, the Pistons, led by Grant, were on the rise.

That season, Grant emerged as one of basketball's brightest stars, even upstaging Michael Jordan as the leading vote-getter for the **All-Star Game**—again. Grant led the league in **triple-doubles**. His season averages were 20 points, 10 **rebounds**, and 7 assists per game.

   The following season Grant and the Pistons were even better. They hit the 50-win mark with a 54-28 record. They were a team to look out for. But in the **playoffs**, the team lost another hard-fought series, this time to the Atlanta Hawks.

Grant Hill driving to the hoop.

A Gold Medal

After Grant's second year in the **NBA**, he didn't take a break in the summer. Instead he joined a group of NBA **All-Stars** as part of "Dream Team II." The Dream Team was the 1996 United States Men's Olympic Basketball Team.

It was a dream come true for Grant to be a part of this special team and represent his country. Some of the basketball greats that Grant was playing alongside included Charles Barkley, Anfernee Hardaway, Shaquille O'Neal, Scottie Pippen, and Hakeem Olajuwon.

In the first game of the **Olympics**, the Dream Team took on Argentina and beat them badly. In the Gold Medal Game, the Dream Team beat Yugoslavia. In between, the Dream Team never had a problem.

Grant played great ball but was just happy to be a part of such an awesome experience. With millions of people watching all over the world, Grant had never felt so nervous.

After the Dream Team received their Gold Medal, the United States National Anthem was played. Grant was feeling every type of emotion. The fans at the stadium in Atlanta were waving flags and clapping very loudly. Grant smiled, waved, gushed, and even teared up. It was one of the proudest moments of his life.

Grant Hill playing for the United States Olympic Dream Team.

Change The Game

Grant is truly a role model. He is a great player and a great person. Grant wrote an autobiography called *Change the Game*, which is about his entire life from child to adult. It also is about making a difference in the world, not just on the basketball court, but in life. If you have the chance, he says, make a difference in life and try to change the game for the better.

Grant believes in being a role model to young people. Grant had many role models while growing up. He had his father and mother who were always there for him. He also looked up to **athletes** such as Muhammad Ali, Arthur Ashe, Magic Johnson, Larry Bird, and Roger Staubach. These were people who made a difference by working hard and being good role models. Just like Grant, these people changed the game, on and off the field, for the better.

Grant's biggest concern is for kids to try many different types of activities. Not everyone can be a **professional**

athlete. Grant worked hard in school, played many different sports, and even played the piano. To this day Grant still plays the piano and is very good. He even played the piano on the David Letterman Show. The whole audience stood and clapped for Grant.

Grant's main emphasis in life is that everyone should have something to fall back on. He constantly tells kids to have a second parachute. If you jump out of a plane and the first parachute doesn't work you need to have a second one. Grant's second parachute was his excellent education. He knew that if he didn't make it in sports he wouldn't have to worry because he worked hard in school and could find a great job outside of sports.

Grant tells kids to have a dream and work hard for it but also to have something else. The danger is not wanting to be like your heroes. The danger is in forgetting everything else to chase that dream. He goes on to say that a dream is just that: something to shoot for. Arms in the sky, feet planted in reality.

King of the Hill

Grant is King of the Hill because he worked hard. He has made it because he remembered school and always listened and respected his teachers, coaches, and parents.

Grant makes sure that others have opportunities too. He gives his time and money to various **charities**. He especially helps **underprivileged** children.

Grant has **contracted** with FILA Shoes to fund summer camps for basketball and academics for inner-city youngsters. At these camps Grant speaks to the children about the importance of school. Through these programs, Grant helps kids become better students and **athletes**, giving them confidence and tools to achieve their goals.

Grant also donates to many charities. In fact, he is giving all of the money he makes from his book to children's charities for education.

Grant knows that he had a wonderful life growing up. He also worked hard and made himself a better **athlete** and student. Grant could have sat back and lived off the successes of his mother and father, but he never wanted that. In fact, he never wanted people to know that he was the son of a famous person.

Through hard work, determination, practice, studying, and listening to others, Grant has become King of the Hill.

Grant Hill going in for the slam.

Glossary

All-Star - A player who is voted by fans as the best player at his position in a given year.

All-Star Game - A game played at the half way point of the season between the best players from the Eastern and Western conference.

Athlete - Someone who is physically skilled and talented at sports.

Autograph - A signature of someone famous.

Center - An offensive player who plays in the middle closest to the basket. They are usually the tallest player on the team.

Championship - The final basketball game or series to determine the best team.

Charities - A fund or organization for helping the poor, the sick, and the helpless.

College - The school you go to after high school for higher education to earn a degree.

Contract - A legal document signed by a player that states how much money they will get paid to play and how many years they will play for a particular team. It is also a document that says a player will wear a particular shoe, clothes, or endorse products and do commercials.

Draft - An event held where NBA teams choose amateur players to be on their team. After the lottery teams pick, it then goes according to team record with the best team getting the last pick.

Freshman - A first year high school or college student.

Graduate - Finishing school and getting your diploma.

National Basketball Association (NBA) - A professional basketball league in the United States and Canada consisting of the Eastern and Western Conferences.

NCAA - This stands for the National Collegiate Athletic Association, which oversees all athletic competition at the college level.

Olympics - Athletic contests held every four years in a different country. Athletes from many nations compete in them.
Playoffs - Games played by the best teams after the regular season to determine a champion.
Professional - Playing a sport and getting paid for it.
Rebound - Getting the ball after a missed shot.
Rookie - A first year player in a sport.
Rookie of the Year - An award given to the best rookie player in that particular year.
Scholarship - A money award used to pay for school given to someone for their particular skills.
Senior - A fourth year high school or college student.
Triple-Double - recording double figures (10 or more) in the three categories of scoring, assists, and rebounding.
Underprivileged - People who are poorer than most.
Varsity - The best team in high school or college sports.

PASS IT ON

Tell Others Something Special About Your Favorite Sports or Athletes

What makes your favorite athlete awesome? Do you think you have a chance to be an Awesome Athlete? Tell us about your favorite plays, tournaments, and anything else that has to do with sports. We want to hear from you!

To get posted on ABDO & Daughters website E-mail us at "sports@abdopub.com"

Index

A

Ali, Muhammad   26
Argentina   24
Ashe, Arthur   26
Atlanta Hawks   23

B

Barkley, Charles   24
Bird, Larry   26
Blue Devil   13, 14, 18, 19

C

Clinton, Hillary   6

D

Dallas Cowboys   6, 9
Dallas Mavericks   21
Dallas, Texas   6
Davis, Brian   15
Detroit Pistons   4, 20
Dream Team   4, 24, 25
Duke   13, 14, 15, 18

F

Final Four   18, 19

G

Georgetown   13

H

Hardaway, Anfernee   24
Hill, Calvin   6, 7
Hill, Thomas   15
Hurley, Bobby   15

J

Johnson, Magic   26
Jordan, Michael   13, 22

K

Kentucky   18
Kidd, Jason   21
Krzyzewski, Mike   14

L

Laettner, Christian   15, 18
Letterman, David   27
Louisville   13

M

Michigan   13

N

National Basketball Association (NBA)   4, 19, 20, 21, 24
NCAA tournament   18, 19
NFL   6
North Carolina   13

O

Olajuwon, Hakeem   24
Orlando Magic   22

P

Parks, Cherokee   15
Pippen, Scottie   24

R

Rookie of the Year   4, 6, 21

S

Smith, Dean   13
state tournament   12
Staubach, Roger   7, 9, 26
Super Bowl   6

T

Thompson, John   13

U

UCLA   13

V

Virginia   9

W

Washington D.C.   6, 9
Wellesley College   6

Y

Yale University   6
Yugoslavia   24